ROGER DAYTON

Koyukuk

Roger Dayton

Koyukuk

Copyright © Yukon-Koyukuk School District 1981

Produced by: Yukon-Koyukuk School District of Alaska

Superintendent: Joe Cooper

Assistant Superintendent-Instruction: Fred Lau

IEA/JOM Coordinator: Don Kratzer

Editing and Interviews by:
　　Curt Madison
　　Yvonne Yarber

Photographs and cover illustration by: Curt Madison (unless otherwise noted)

Materials collected during November of 1978 in Koyukuk, Alaska

Project funded by the following sources:
　　Indian Education Grant #0553A
　　Johnson-O'Malley Grant #EOC 1420-1834

ISBN 0-88839-067-X

No part of this book may be reproduced by any means without written permission of the publisher.

Published by:
HANCOCK HOUSE PUBLISHERS
1431 Harrison Avenue, Blaine, WA, U.S.A. 98230
HANCOCK HOUSE PUBLISHERS LTD.
19313 Zero Avenue, Surrey, B.C., Canada V3S 5J9

Regional School Board:
　　Don Honea, Sr. - Chairman
　　Wally Carlo - Vice Chairman
　　Ivan Sipary - Treasurer
　　Vera Strack - Secretary/Clerk
　　Fred Attla, Sr.
　　Eddie Bergman
　　William Dayton
　　Pat McCarty
　　Eleanor Sweetsir

Cataloging in Publication Data

Dayton, Roger
　Roger Dayton, Koyukuk

　(Alaska Series)
　ISBN 0-88839-067-X

　1. Dayton, Roger. 2. Koyukon Indians - Biography - Juvenile literature. 3. Indians of North America - Alaska - Biography - Juvenile literature. I. Title. II. Series.
　E99.K79D39　j970.004'97　C80-091248-9

Cover

Roger Dayton, November 1978 in Koyukuk, Alaska.

Title Page

A part of Roger's family at fish camp, Bishop Mountain 1980.
Front Row: Frankie Dayton, Kathy Jane Dayton holding April One Dayton, Madeline Solomon holding Stewart James Solomon, Lilly Ann Dayton holding Elvin James Dayton, Dewaine Dayton, Glen Kriska.
Row Two: Elaine Solomon, Catherine Dayton, Jennie and Carrie Ann Pelkola, Kaki Dayton, Hughie Kriska Jr.
Back Row: Dorothy Dayton, Oscar Dayton, Martha Nelson, Edith Kriska, Tommy Kriska holding David Charles Dayton whose knit cap is showing, Eleanor Kriska, Roger Dayton.

PRINTED IN CANADA

A Note From A Linguist

As you read through this autobiography you will notice a style and a diction you may not have seen before in print. This is because it is an oral, storytelling style. This autobiography has been compiled from many hours of taped interviews. As you read you should listen for the sound of the spoken voice. While it has not been possible to show all the rhythms and nuances of the speaker's voice, much of the original style has been kept. If possible you should read aloud and use your knowledge of the way the old people speak to recapture the style of the original.

This autobiography has been written in the original style for three reasons. First, the original style is a kind of dramatic poetry that depends on pacing, succinctness, and semantic indirectness for its narrative impact. The original diction is part and parcel of its message and the editors have kept that diction out of a deep respect for the person represented in this autobiography.

The second reason for keeping the original diction is that it gives a good example of some of the varied richness of the English language. English as it is spoken in many parts of the world and by many different people varies in style and the editors feel that it is important for you as a reader to know, understand and respect the wide resources of this variation in English.

The third reason for writing in the original style is that this style will be familiar to many of you who will read this book. The editors hope that you will enjoy reading something in a style that you may never have seen written before even though you have heard it spoken many times.

Ron Scollon
Alaska Native Language Center
University of Alaska
Fairbanks
July 1979

Acknowledgments

Many thanks to everyone who continues to help with this project. Special appreciation is due Bob Maguire who concieved and midwived these first few books, Ron Scollon who wrote the note on language style, and Bea Hagen whose attuned ear gave us clear transcripts. Joe Cooper, Superintendent of Yukon Koyukuk School District; and, Fred Lau, Assistant Superintendent-Instruction; and, Don Kratzer, Indian Education Coordinator, have provided generous administrative support. Finally, this project could not continue without the interest in local curriculum by the members of the Yukon-Koyukuk School District Regional Board.

All royalties from the sale of this book go to the Yukon-Koyukuk School District for the production of more biographies.

This is the first printing of this book. Please notify us of any errors so they can be corrected in future printings.

Table of Contents

A Note From A Linguist   5
Acknowledgments   6
Foreword   9
Maps   10
Introduction   11
Glossary   12

CHAPTER ONE   STORIES THROUGH THE GENERATIONS

The First Born   14
A Trip To Meet the Coast People   14
Grandfather's Friends   18
Work of the Medicine Man   20
Remembering On and Off Yet   21
Koyukuk   22

CHAPTER TWO   HOLY CROSS

Not Much School   26
We Made Our Own Fun   30
Fourth of July   31
Games   33
Visiting   33
Coming Home   35

CHAPTER THREE   LEARNING THE OUTDOOR LIFE

Teaching of Sons   38
I Liked to Listen   41
Real Trapping With My Old Man   42
Springtime   44
Flood   45
Caching Ducks and Geese   47
Fishing   47

CHAPTER FOUR   I WAS YOUNG

Airplanes   50
Service   53
Gambling   55
Dog Race   56
Bear   57
Loose Dogs   58

CHAPTER FIVE	PAYING BILLS	
The Same Life		60
Fishing		61
Out With Annie and the Kids		64
Big Bills		66
Dominic Vernetti		67
Cannery Work		70

CHAPTER SIX	KOYUKUK 1979	
Teaching Kids About Outdoor Life		74
Water In Koyukuk		80
Signs of Luck		81
INDEX		85

Foreword

Roger Dayton - Koyukuk is the seventh in a series of autobiographies of people who live in the eleven villages serviced by the Yukon-Koyukuk School District. These books are designed for upper level elementary students living in rural Alaska although they may well captivate readers of any age.

Most school materials in Alaska come from Outside and mention Alaska peripherally, if at all. We need not be described as a "Barren wasteland" on the edge of the real world. We are a center of a rich and varied but, unfortunately, neglected culture. We hope to bring home some relevance of curriculum through this series.

This story of Roger Dayton offers students the opportunity to take a closer look at home and to study some of the changes that have taken place in a historically short span of time. It is written in six chapters to allow easy breaking points for discussion and activities. There are suggested student activities for this book available from the Yukon-Koyukuk School District office, Nenana, Alaska 99760.

This book has been written in the language style of the story teller. As his speech is like that of many students, it may allow easy reading. For others it is an introduction to a language that has evolved since the recent coming of Outside people to Native Alaskan land.

This book is by no means a definitive work. It should be viewed as a beginning point for teachers in classrooms throughout the Interior.

Curt Madison and Yvonne Yarber
Manley Hot Springs, Alaska, 1981.

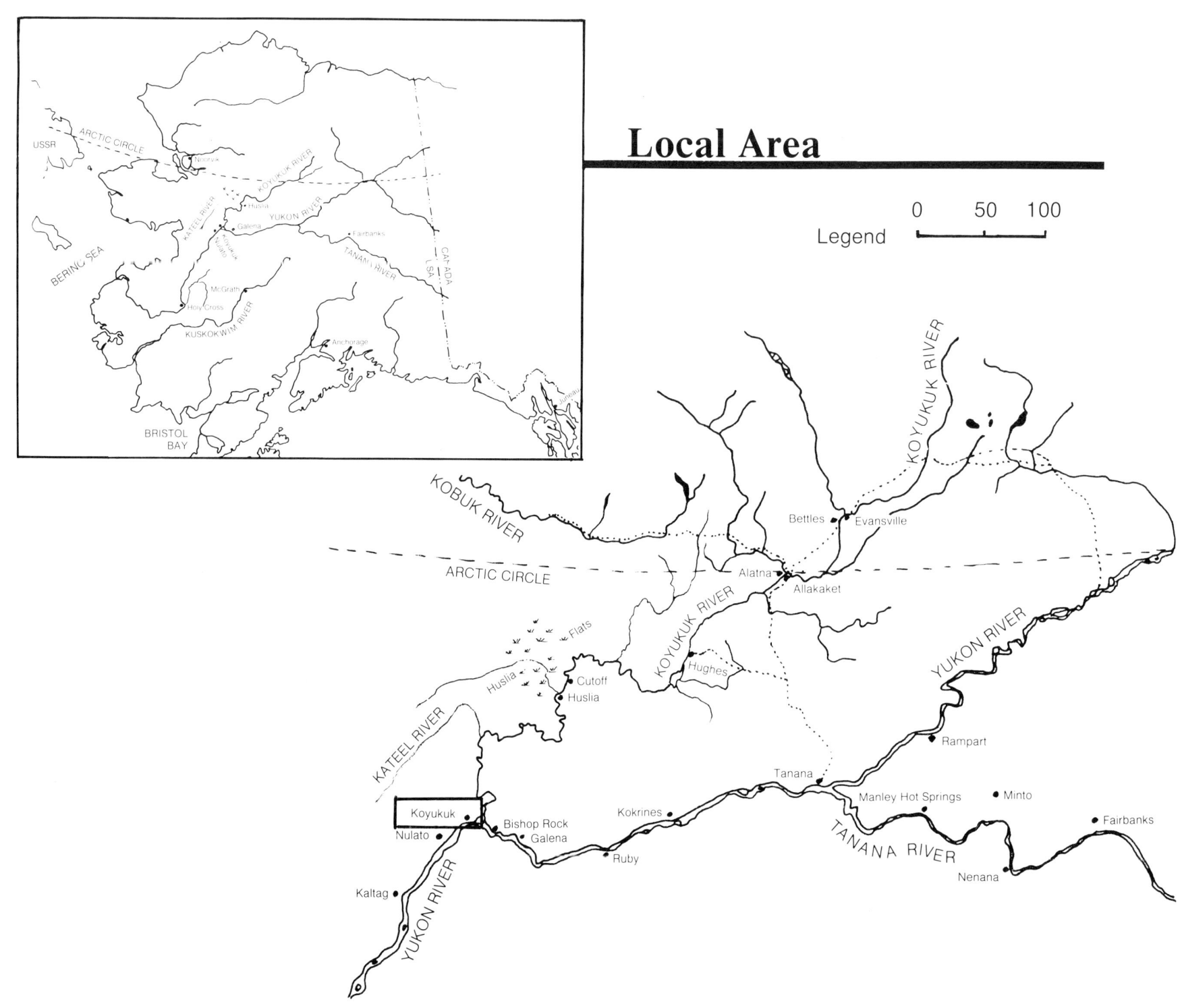

Introduction

Roger Dayton lives in Koyukuk, an Athabaskan village at the mouth of the Koyukuk River on the Yukon. He spends his winters there working as a maintenance man for the school. In the summer Roger and his family stay in their cabin at Bishop Mountain as do his mother, many of his brothers and sisters, and their families. He also fishes commercially with a fishwheel on the Yukon downriver from Koyukuk. His mother, Madeline Solomon says of Roger, "Once he gets started with the fishwheel he never stops. All day he's just back and forth working on fish."

Roger had little to say of his own accomplishments and talents. About this book he comments, "I said what I could to show a life."

Koyukuk Village.

Glossary

bingle—tokens given in place of money as change when goods were purchased. In the early 1900s storeowners along the Yukon used them as a means of getting customers to come back to their store.

Holy Cross—originally a Native village named Anilukgtakpak (Zagoskin 1844). In 1886 a Jesuit mission and school were established. In 1899 a post office under the name Koserefski was established and in 1912 the name was changed to Holy Cross to coincide with the mission. The mission school was later taken over by the State of Alaska as a public school.

Koyukuk—(pop 128) originally listed as an Eskimo village and trading post by Ivan Petroff in his 1880 census. It is actually a Koyukon, Athabaskan village. A post office opened for two years in 1898 and then reopened in 1933. Present Koyukuk includes an air field, water plant, laundrymat, and showers, school, telephone and television transmitted by satellite.

longshoring—loading and unloading freight from ships and barges.

scow—large flat bottomed boat.

Everyone working at their own table. The poles behind Eleanor are for repairing the fish wheel anchored at the bluff. Bishop Mountain, June 1980.

CHAPTER ONE   Stories Through the Generations

The First Born

I was born in the month of September, the year 1921. Right there in Nulato, Alaska. The village was established long before that. Hard to say who delivered me. He was a doctor from the States. Anyway, he named me after his father Roger. It was in the old hospital that used to be down there. It's all torn down now.

From what I heard I was premature, that's born a little too early. A lot of old people was concerned about my mother and me. That's what my father used to tell me. But then I guess I pull through.

My mother used to live at Nulato. Cecelia Williams adopted her down there. My father used to be from up here at Koyukuk. He used to visit my mother down there now and then, he'd court her. Shortly before I was born in that hospital, they got married. Then I suppose they moved up here to Koyukuk. I was the first. The next brother I had was three years younger than I was.

Standing: Roger Dayton, Jennie Pelkola, Franklin Dayton; sitting: Eleanor Kriska, Madeline Solomon, Elaine Solomon.

A Trip to Meet The Coast People

Soon as I started remembering was when I was about three or four years old. We was taking a trip to the coast just before Christmas. Of course lot of these Eskimo people from the coast used to trap close to us on the Huslia River. And then we happened to be trapping close to them on this side of the ridge there.

They invited my old man over for Christmas and New Year's. From that time I start remembering. It was an interesting trip but it was just sort of a dream to me now and then. We went to Noorvik for the New Year's and I remember they had a torch lit and were walking around with it celebrating New Year's.

Like I said, it was just like a dream to me, off and on. I remember coming back on a high mountain. The wind was blowing pretty strong there. A fellow named Basel was with us. He was on what you call a gee pole and I guess I was riding way in the sleigh. My mother and father were walking behind. I suppose we were coming back home.

Later on I hear old stories about when people used to kill one another. You know, people from the coast and people from the Interior. There's some stories of in the spring when people start going out for beaver hunting. They used to use just bow and arrows for beaver hunting then. And whoever wants to go and rob somebody else would camp on the side of a hill. Then when he saw campfire off in the distance he knew there was somebody there.

So he'd start toward that place and hide not far from there and when he thinks that fellow goes to bed he'd sneak up and either shoot him with an arrow or club him. Sometimes this fellow he wants to rob just didn't have anything at all. Sometimes they used to do it just for a can of tobacco. Kill one another.

I wouldn't call that a war, it's just taking place between two men not from the same village. Just for little stuff. In that way they used to kill one another quite a bit. People from one village hardly fought among themselves. Between villages they used to fight quite a bit, but in them days they used nothing but spears and arrows.

The things they obtained from the Russians was this tobacco, those square Chinese matches and maybe an old fashioned ax. I guess they learned how to smoke and valued those things. And then sometimes if an enemy thinks the other guy has something from the Russians like a can of tobacco he just kills him for it. But that was long time before our time.

One time in the fall of 1935 my old man and me were going up the Koyukuk River. A fellow by the name of Wilfred Evans was taking us up because we had no boat of our own at the time. My old man mentioned this old bunker that people used to have for protection against any enemies. He explained how villages used to fight quite a bit among themselves.

Wilfred wanted to see this bunker so we stopped there and went up the bank. Maybe about a couple of hundred yards back in the woods we came to the place of this underground bunker made of logs. I'd say it was just above the mouth of the Kateel River. Up on the Koyukuk River, the right hand side going up.

That bunker wasn't too big. Maybe about twelve feet square with a tunnel going to the next place. The next place was another, the same size and covered over with logs too. There was no windows. Just little holes big enough to shoot arrows through. It was just so high off the ground so they could shoot at their enemy.

When we saw that bunker part of it was caved in. The logs was pretty well rotten and the floor was only about three feet deep. Because as the years came along it keep filling up with mud. Before, they could stand up inside there. I guess they were pretty well protected that way. I suppose those bunkers indicated that they used to fight quite a bit among themselves.

I guess stories came down through the generations. I just know what my father used to tell us. My father tell us one incident where people from the Koyukuk River went towards the Huslia River. That's toward the coast. One night they were camping, about three or four of them. And late at night when they still have campfire going all of a sudden somebody threw something like a big stick at them from out of the camp.

Right away they found out what that guy was up to. So they whispered among themselves what to do you know, they'll pretend that they'll go to sleep and let that fellow sneak into camp. Well, they all went to bed, then this fellow, he sneak closer to camp. Then everybody jump up and made for him. They grabbed hold of him and asked him where he was from. He said he was from the coast, he was an Eskimo.

They made him their prisoner and guarded him all night till it get daylight. Morning time they asked him why he attacked them. He said he had nothing to eat and couldn't help but do that. He said he was only trying to drive the men away from the camp so he could get a hold of the grub.

They could have killed him there. It was just easy, he was only one. It happened that he was a loner and I guess these people sort of feel sorry for him. They told him, "We'll give you grub enough to go home. And you'd better go home, just the way you came." So, this fellow promised that he was going to do that.

There was an old fellow among these other people. He said "Wait a minute, I want to remember that fellow there. Cut off one side of his ear so we'll know who he is." They did just that before they let him go. That's to remember who he was. Then he got back home and people notice that one side of his ear is missing. They asked what

happened to his ear and he told them all about it. They told him, "You're lucky they didn't kill you." And that's one incident my old man used to tell us about.

That trip we made over to Noorvik was years later. We took that trip over there in 1925. Like I told you, these people from the coast, they invited us over there. They were pretty friendly over there. And my father didn't even mention any bitter feelings so these wars must have been cured years before.

Grandfather's Friends

My grandfather used to know these older people, same age as him. They got to be pretty good friends and in that way they were all friendly towards us. He used to trap and hunt close to where these people from the coast used to hunt and trap, on the Huslia Flats. That's how he got to know them.

This Uncle Albert told me about that just lately. He told me he was out on the Huslia Flats camping with his father, my grandfather. Uncle Albert was twelve or thirteen years old. And in them days they used to chop out beaver what's got no water. That water in the fall drains away from the lake. They're easy to get then.

One morning they went out to work some on this beaver house. This uncle of mine happened to look down the lake and he seen two guys coming towards him. And the way they greet each other is the holler at your first, "Hello" to see if you'd answer in a friendly way. If you answer in a friendly way they'd come right to you.

My grandfather recognized them right away, these two guys. Oh, were they happy to see each other. Then my grandfather invited them to their camp. Made a pot of soup, bear soup. Fed them everything. Dry fish. They talked all night and the way he tells it, they didn't sleep at all. And they'd sing for each other you know. They'd sing in their language and my grandfather would sing for them. They never seen one another for quite a few years but that way they sort of got together again.

My grandfather and these two other guys never slept all night until noontime. Then finally these two guys from the coast had to go. My grandfather gave them some meat, little grub, little dry fish. They'd exchange grub. Like people from the coast would bring over seal oil and blubber. They become acquainted like that.

That's the way my uncle told it, Albert, that's my grandfather's youngest son. He's just about ten years older than I am. I'm fifty-seven, he must be about sixty-seven. My grandfather's name was Tom Dayton.

Old Man Stickman in his birchbark hunting canoe. Photo by Father Jette, Nulato. c. 1910

Work of The Medicine Man

My uncle used to tell me other things too. My grandfather and my father never talked too much about what medicine man performed. My uncle used to tell me about it. That's how I know about one that cured my father. My father got sick, didn't eat and just laid in bed. He was between twenty and twenty-five, didn't have no appetite and my grandfather didn't know what to do about it. He said he didn't eat for twenty-one days. He was just skin and bones.

Then my grandfather suggested something about a medicine man down at Nulato. It was all right with my father. So my grandfather went and talked this over down there. After awhile this medicine man came up. Old Joseph Stickman. I don't know exactly what sort of medicine he performed on my father. Of course he sang but then I wouldn't understand what he did. It's sort of hard to believe, but he cured my father. Then my grandfather had to pay him for that. Whatever he asked for or was satisfied with. I suppose it was money. We ourselves, we don't believe much in that. But then, when older people tell us about that, I suppose you have to believe some of it. If it works you can't argue with that.

There used to be lots of them medicine people, people from other villages. I used to hear lots about them. Of course there used to be one that lived here. His name was Andrew Pilot, the husband of that old Sally Pilot. And talking about medicine men I can tell you a story that happened up Ruby.

This Andrew Pilot and this medicine man from down at Nulato were both at Ruby one time for potlatch and events like dog races and snowshoe races. There was a White man up there. He used to have an awful good team and everyone knew he was going to win the prize. I believe his name was Dave Walters.

Well you know how it is, the people around here, they favor their own people. So these two medicine men get together. They asked one another, "Well partner, what we going to do?" And this younger man, Andrew Pilot told him, "Well, do what you want. Because maybe you got stronger medicine than I got."

So, this Dave Walters there that had a good team started out. He was catching up one team, pass the team, and pass another team. Pretty soon a crow came from behind. Black crow, and he went over the leader and that crow just turn off towards the shore over there.

You know what dogs will do. They just took the trail after that crow and lost a lot of time that way. That fella didn't win. Somebody else won the race.

That's a strange thing, a crow just happened to fly over that fast team there. Just over the head of that leader for so long and then turn off. I guess that was the work of the medicine man.

Remembering On and Off Yet

And then, remembering was like off and on yet. I remember the next brother I had, John Jr., being born in one of the camps up there and, of course, an old lady, Miss Old Toby, delivered him. It was in the month of January and my folks were coming down to sell their furs.

Everybody else was doing that, too. Whenever they think they've got enough fur they come down, or if they're short of groceries or something. Everybody was trapping. There used to be camps about every ten or fifteen miles apart in those years. All the way from here to Huslia.

There was couple of traders here and people sold their furs to them. They didn't sell their furs to anybody else in those years, just try to pay back their bills to the storekeepers. And after they settle down here, they celebrate for a little and then they were ready to go back to camp and start trapping again. It went on like that for year after year.

After trapping the people would come back down in April and then move out again to do some muskrat hunting. Around the first part of June they'd all move back down here. Some would do pretty good with muskrat, and they were only about fifty to seventy-five cents a piece in those years.

I remember going out with my mother, sitting behind her in the canoe. I was never still you know. Everytime muskrat was swimming towards her, I'd move to look at that muskrat so the canoe wasn't steady. Sometimes she'd shoot and miss the muskrat. She'd sort of scold me for moving that canoe, tell me to keep still. I suppose all the kids were that way.

Koyukuk

Whenever we weren't out at camp we would stay in Koyukuk. I never heard of how that place got started. Nicholia Slough was the first place. It was in the 1850's they had a village there. There was no village here at Koyukuk at that time. Maybe a few places people could hunt and trap but not much down this way.

Nicholia Slough got its name because an old man used to live

Dominic Vernetti's old generator house and warehouses.

there. An old bachelor named Nicholia. That slough runs out from the Koyukuk River all the way out below Galena. They call it Bear Creek, this creek below Galena, but Nicholia Slough runs into Bear Creek. Sometimes people from Galena, they'd make a short cut that way if they want to go up the Koyukuk River. That would be in the spring when the water is high. They go just to hunt or fish.

I don't know when the first cabin was built in Koyukuk. You'd have to ask someone older than I am. But the oldest building was put up around World War I. A frame house down a little below the village that's here now. There was a few Army men stationed here, Signal Corp men. The missionaries wrote some stories about them. They had a wireless down here they call Koyukuk Station.

They had this big tower, high steel tower. The one at Nulato was there for awhile. But that was done away with around 1937 or '38. In the book about my mother there's a picture of that tower. That Koyukuk Station closed down sometime in the twenties I think. We'd find a lot of that telegraph line along the hill and gather it for fishwheels and whatever we wanted to work with.

There used to be a telephone too. I don't know how it would cross the Yukon River. I know it ran from here all the way to Kaltag. I suppose it ran all the way up the Yukon because during this diphtheria run of 1925 they used to phone from village to village to see where the serum was, where the dog musher was. But I don't know how it crossed the river to Ruby. You know Ruby is on the other side of the river. Rampart is the only other one on the other side of the main Yukon River until you get to Circle. All the old Native villages are on the north bank.

I remember where the wire ran across the Koyukuk River, there used to be two long poles. One on each side about a mile up from the mouth with the wire stretched out between. Maybe they put two or three logs together for one pole. I remember they were pretty high. Maybe it fell over between 1940 and '45.

Mostly storekeepers had phones in their stores. I remember we had one in our cabin. I remember talking on it when I was a kid. Ours rang just like these present phones. And I stood my chair against the wall. I picked up the receiver and there was somebody talking to one another. I was just a kid and I tell them, "Aw, shut up," and hung up.

I remember one other time talking to my mother. It was the spring of 1940 and telephones were still working between here and

Kaltag. She took a trip down with dogteam and I stayed here. She called me from Kaltag and asked me what I needed, what the store here didn't have like seal oil and blubber. She asked me how much I'd like to have and I told her about an empty lard can full plus some other stuff.

That's the way I remember talking on this old-type telephone. You crank it up to ring it you know. So many rings each place. If it's three rings it was for Dominic Vernetti's Store. One or two rings for next door. They all had different number of rings. I don't know why my folks had that phone. Just to talk to other people I suppose. In them years the fur was plentiful and they were pretty good price. Maybe they just wanted to buy one.

Marion Huntington's house in Koyukuk. November 1978.

CHAPTER TWO Holy Cross

Not Much School

I didn't have much schooling in my life. We were mostly out trapping. When we came back out to Koyukuk, what little time we spent here, I used to go to school. But that time was too short. We didn't learn anything at all here. My parents sent me to Holy Cross for five years and I went up as far as third grade and then no more after that. We move out in the falltime before freeze up and stay out there all winter. Just two or three families stayed in town and lot of times there wasn't enough kids to have school.

My parents sent us down to Holy Cross, two of us, in the summer of 1930. Me and my younger brother, Oscar. He was three years younger than me. They made arrangements with the missionaries there that we were going to be there for five years. When the five years was up they sent for us. My brother passed away just a few months before we were set to come back home. He got sick somehow. I don't know what kind of sickness he got. He was sick for about a month and then he passed away.

When we first got there my brother and I used to talk our language quite a bit, but the missionaries didn't like that. They couldn't understand us and they might think we're talking about them. They made us speak English so they'd understand what we're saying. They'd remind us not to speak our language, but we never got punished for

The main alter at Holy Cross Mission.

Early Holy Cross Mission Brothers and Fathers (l-r): Mr. Rene; Brother Bartholomew Mark, S.J.; Brother Eugene Lefebure, S.J.; Father Joseph Perron, S.J.; Father Luck Lucchese, S.J.; Father Aloysius Robaut, S.J.; Brother Edward Horwedel, S.J.; Brother Constantine (scholastic); Brother Aloysius Markham, S.J.

that. We got punished for fighting and for being lazy. And for answering back or whatever mischief we'd get into.

When you start school there they don't put you in a grade, they start you off with *Primer A*. I went through *Primer A* and *B*, both of them. Then I went to first, second, and third grade. That's the highest I went to — third grade.

There was over two hundred kids down there, so to us that was a lot. We knew just what to expect because my father and mother were down there themselves and they used to talk quite a bit about it. There were rules and regulations and all the kids were alike. There was not love too much for one kid or nothing. The missionaries handled it like that. They didn't favor nobody. I suppose it was good for us. Of course, when we'd get into mischief, they'd discipline us quite a bit and they spanked us.

I got disciplined for answering back. I still remember I got paddling in the mouth for answering back. It hurt so much I still remember that. It wasn't like now, you know, they hardly lick any kid in school anymore. And there's lot of other ways you get punished. Sometimes they make you miss a meal. Sometimes they make you go to bed early.

I spoke very little English when I went to Holy Cross. Then after five years I completely forgot my language up here. When I came back to Koyukuk I couldn't understand even my own father and mother.

There were kids from all over the place in Holy Cross. Some from Fairbanks, some from way down river, some from the Kuskokwim River. All over. Kids from different places spoke among themselves. Like Eskimos among themselves and Natives from here use the language from the Interior. Some of the kids when they were sent there didn't know a word of English. After awhile they'd catch on.

It was like any regular school. Start around nine o'clock and out maybe three o'clock in the afternoon. But they sure make us learn. Oh yes, they make us learn. Mostly about Bible history. Well, it was since missionaries being there. They talked mostly about Bible and the Lord. They see to it that the kids learned. And if they didn't learn they got disciplined.

Sometimes instead of being graduated they'd put you back. Anybody that couldn't learn. There was some kids like that. And they were year after year in the same grade. They just couldn't learn anything. It was just natural I guess.

Sometimes we'd get spanking pretty hard for smoking. I used to get into that. Maybe when we'd take a walk down to the village we'd pick up butts here and there. That way we obtained tobacco. And the bigger boys were allowed to smoke. Camel, Lucky Strike, or whatever the bigger boys give us. Like if we gave them some candy they'd give us cigarettes. It was a pretty good trade but of course we'd get punished for it. We got pretty hard spanking for that with a strap about quarter inch thick. They make us put down our pants and whoa! That really hurts. A leather strap.

A lush just caught by dipping for it under the ice.

We Made Our Own Fun

We would make our own fun. We used our tools to make toy airplanes or wooden boats or sleighs just to play with. We made our own tools and we found some discarded ones too. Like an old file, old pliers, maybe an old chisel. I had a cigar box full with them old things. That's what I brought from Holy Cross. But then after I came home I suppose I threw them away.

Nails for the awl we make out of box wires. There used to be a lot of that come to the Mission. Butter, gas, near everything used to come in wooden boxes with wires wrapped around. That's the way they were packed.

One boy used to make pretty good airplanes. They sent some out to Juneau for an exhibition and he used to get first prize for that he was so good at it. Martin Ott was his name. He was fifteen or sixteen and a good carpenter. They gave him the job of replacing windows. He could really handle this putty. So good it looked like it was right from the factory. Whatever he did we used to do the same. He made a wood airplane with lumber and skis. A bunch of us would pull it up the hill and he'd get in it and slide down.

He made a coaster and put a propeller in the front of it. When he came down the hill it would turn fast. He was the first one to do that.

Raising the fish trap to empty out the lush. Holy Cross Mission.

Fourth of July

Fourth of July was just fourth of July. We never got ready for it. The missionaries would get some prizes ready like an apple, or candy bar. Small things. We had swimming contests and diving contest. Of course the bigger boys were always first on that because the younger boys just couldn't swim. The lake was right behind the village. It was about a quarter mile long by about hundred yards wide.

We had foot races, and wheelbarrow races, three-legged races and baseball. I was in foot race quite a bit but I never did win first. Sometimes I was second or third and maybe I'd get a handful of candy for that. Just a short race for the younger kids maybe about fifty yards. Bigger kids went hundred yards.

Wheelbarrow race was, one kid used to hold your legs and you'd walk with your arms. The line was fifty feet away. When you get there you swing around and the other kid would get on his hands, you grab his legs and come back. Some kids won quite a bit but I always got beat on that.

Fourth of July was different here in Koyukuk. We had contests like swimming and baseball, running, tug of war, and jumping. You used to run and then you'd leap. Womens used to do a hammering contest. They'd use a log and then they'd all kneel down beside it and then they were given so many nails apiece. Hit 'em with a hammer. All the way in. Maybe they were given five or six nails. Whoever drove them all first was the winner. Womens did that not men.

Of course, there were canoe races, boat races. They'd take all the

Fishing under the ice with a trap at Holy Cross. Notice all the lush in the snow. Lush livers were most people's favorite food.

Dip netting for fish at Holy Cross. The two men have nets on the ends of their poles.

canoe racers across the river right around the point. They'd make them all line up just like in the foot race. Whenever they give the signal the canoes would start across. All kind of people used to be winners in that. Just women among themselves and men among themselves.

Before the Fourth of July, they used to go around and gather up money for the prizes. Collect a dollar or two from each person. Mostly in coins. If you won ten dollars they give you a ten dollar bill, five they give you five. There was no single dollar bills in them years just coins.

Games

We'd just play all sorts of games, just make them up, whatever came to our minds. Hide and seek, racing, and football. For football we had a goal on each end and you do mostly kicking. If you ever happen to get that ball through a goal, then you'd win. Just run back and forth, but I never played too much of that. Mostly old people played that.

We used to play this catch can. You'd stand with your foot close to the bank on a can and you'd count. All the other children would be behind the houses. You'd have to name everyone of them kids who they are and where they're hiding. If you make a mistake naming the wrong kid, they're allowed to kick the can over the bank. And then you'd have to walk down the bank and get the can. Sometimes they'd kick the can right in the water and you'd still have to get it and try over again. Right now they play mostly this marbles whenever the ground is cleared in the spring. And as the time comes along they play this basketball. You never see a game of catch can anymore.

Visiting

There were families living in Holy Cross village; Demientieffs, Andrews, Edwards, Walkers, and some other people that I don't remember. Mostly the people from the village came to visit the school when they visited their kids. And every weekend the kids right from Holy Cross visited their folks. They boarded at the school but every weekend were permitted to visit their folks. I visted our relatives once and they gave us some candies and then we were sent back to the Mission. That was around 1933.

We'd get pretty lonely for home all through the five years that we were there. Kids didn't like the place. There were too much rules and regulations and we didn't like that.

James Walker's floating store and boat tied up at the bank in Holy Cross.

Coming Home

When it was time to go home I was happy like anybody else. I was thirteen and like any thirteen-year-old kid I had no plans. I was just glad to be getting home. Then like I say when I came back home I couldn't understand our own Native language. I just completely forgot.

And people were so different. They were not religious. And we used to have a lot of fun down there at Holy Cross, laugh at every little thing. People weren't like that around here. Of course I didn't know any better so sometimes I'd laugh at somebody. I couldn't help it because I was down there for five years. I learned that from down there and when I came back up here, I started to behave the same way as when I was at Holy Cross. I was criticized for that.

As I grew older I got out of it. That's one thing about it when you're at the Mission for so long you just completely forget about your own home. Just how they make their living and the language. When I came home I forgot how to hunt, and as simple as snaring rabbits I didn't do too good. My mother had to teach me that. I had to learn about this life all over again.

Some of them were down there for thirty-five years. They were orphans. They had no place to go to, no folks to come back to, so they just stayed at the Mission. This one fellow, Charlie Apostolik, my mother knows him, they're about the same age. He's the one that spent his time there for thirty-five years. He had no home and he got so used to the Mission that he just stayed there. When they did away with the

Ivan Demientieff, rowing, and Charlie Apostolick with king salmon for Holy Cross Mission.

Mission I guess he stayed right at Holy Cross in the village. He didn't move away. Last time I saw him he was up this way with James Walker in 1948. They came up to Galena to get bunch of lumber, army buildings they tore down, and some machinery.

Charlie Apostolik used to have quite a bit of fun with the boys. He was much older and we used to all gang up on him and wrestle. And he used to pull a lot of tricks on us and that way everybody liked him.

When I left Holy Cross in 1935, I came up on the steamer *Nenana*. It's on the bank in Fairbanks now as a museum. I came back on that. There was deep water in front of Koyukuk then, no bar like now. They came right straight across and let me off right here.

I knew the captain because he was an old timer, Captain Adams. He used to pilot these boats long before I ever went down. Everybody used to know him. And the purser and his first mate, everybody knew him too, but he was pretty rough on the deckhands. They didn't like him much. Billy Hardnuts was his name. About 1942 they all got layed off and they went to work on the Kuskokwim River. I got stationed in McGrath in the service for nine months and that's where I saw them again. Captain Adams was still captain, the engineer was still engineer and the first mate was the same. They got so used to that life they couldn't leave it right away. A few years later they all retired and passed away I suppose.

Coming up from Holy Cross we left there about midnight. It took two nights to come up and landed here about middle of the afternoon. My father came down to the boat to meet me. On the way up I walked around the deck, went back on the stern, and looked at that big stern wheel. We weren't allowed to go down on first deck but sometimes I'd sneak down there and take a look at the boilers.

There were a couple other passengers on the boat, a sister and a brother. The brother was about the same age as me and we played quite a bit. We used to run around the deck, trying to catch each other. He invited me into his room. He opened his suitcase and let me see his things he had and I'd do the same thing for him. He had everything because he's from well-to-do family, not wealthy but he had everything. All sorts of clothes, toothbrushes, everything to travel with. But me I didn't have anything at all. My suitcase was given back to me empty.

When we went down there my suitcase was full of clothes. But I outgrew those so in that way my clothes weren't given back to me. I just filled it up with junk. Whatever I had like an old mackinaw coat and old cigar box full of nails, file and old pliers. We used to make our own tools down there like awl. We make it sharp on one end, bend the other end, then work it through wood to make a hole. I had a lot of nails for making awls in the cigar box. That was all I had in my suitcase when I came home. I practically came back with an empty suitcase. Of course, I wouldn't blame whoever took the clothes out of it because I outgrew them. But my suitcase was full when I went down there, shirt, underwear, trousers, handkerchiefs, shirts, toothbrush and some other things that my father and mother put in the suitcase. But not clothes she made. We didn't have no winter clothes along with us when we went down.

That other guy on the steamer *Nenana* was a little younger than me so he probably didn't think too much about it, but I thought he had everything. Maybe he thought I didn't have nothing, but he didn't say.

Hughie Kriska's house, Post Office, and Leonard Huntington's house in Koyukuk 1978.

CHAPTER THREE Learning The Outdoor Life

Teaching the Sons

I learned snaring rabbits from my mother. But if there's a son, it was up to a father to teach most of the things that he's got to learn. He did most of the teaching of sons. It was up to the mother to teach the girls. She'd be teaching them sewing, tanning skins, cutting fish, cooking. Washing I suppose. So they've got their own job to do, father and mother.

Madeline Solomon, Roger's mother, taken by Gabriel Dayton, Roger's son at Bishop Mountain, June 1980.

As I grew along I guess I was doing what all the boys were doing. Sometimes I go with my old man, hunting little ways. Of course he'd tell me this or that. How things were done. Sometimes he'd go after birch and I'd go with him, walking. And I used to play around, doing what any other kids my age would do. Throwing sticks at a squirrel or just running around while he's busy with the birch.

My old man would be hunting birch to build a sleigh. And after he finds the right kind he would hew it and leave it there. Later on he'd get it with a dogteam. It was much easier to get it home that way.

He told me to look for certain kind of birch and test it first. He said to hew it and then tear out that piece and twist it to see if it was just like rubber. "That's the best birch you can get. For snowshoes and sleigh that would last a long time," he used to tell me.

Then as I grew older I used to go out bear hunting with him in the fall when the bears start hibernating but I never used to last too long. I was too young and get tired easily. We would walk a zigzag, not in a straight line. He would try to find a ridge where we think a bear hole was. After I was about eleven or twelve I still go out in the fall with him but I would last longer.

When we hunt bear everybody would string out but we'd all go in one direction. Each person going from right to left, not in a straight line. Keep going wherever he thinks he might find a bear. Then if somebody gets tired, like if any kids are along, they camp early. That's one way of taking care of anybody that gets tired. They don't carry us. We have to walk on our own two legs.

The way they would talk to one another is everybody would carry along an ax. If you would want to know where the next man was,

Roger Dayton with part of his winter moose supply.

Roger and Gabriel sighting across the Yukon River from fish camp. June 1980.

you'd hit a tree. And then when you wanted that person to know that you're going to camp, you hit a tree many times. And then if you're lucky enough to find a bear you holler. That's the only time you'd holler. You didn't talk and laugh unnecessarily either. You just did what you have to do. Just keep moving. You couldn't play around. Otherwise you'd just tire yourself out.

   Usually we'd start about eight or nine o'clock in the morning. Walk till five in the afternoon. Sometimes later. We'd agree where we'd stop for lunch. While we're having lunch we'd agree on where we'd make the camp for the evening, for the night. That way we never got separated.

If we get a bear while we're staying out at camp in the fall we just store it. Cache it away for our own use, whoever's hunting. But if it's close to town or summertime somebody catches a bear, he has a little potlatch or he just pass it around. The meat in summertime don't keep very long. It just spoils. Moose meat, same way.

Sometimes whoever gets the bear and whoever hunts along with them have a regular barbecue. But then not too much of the meat. They bring most of the meat home.

I Liked To Listen

Mostly I hunted with my father and uncle because we all lived in the same camp. Sometimes older people used to go along with us. But that was mostly in the summer with boys about the same age I was, about fourteen, fifteen or a little older. We used to go up the Koyukuk River from a ridge and go all the way back to the summit where the bears were. Most likely we would find them. And when anybody sees a bear they appoint somebody to go ahead and shoot. For instance if any young fellow never shot any game before, they'd give him a chance to shoot. That would be his first kill.

If we were younger boys we never used to let older people work too much, like carrying water, getting all the wood. And then at night they used to tell stories of their old times. We'd sit around the campfire. We'd listen.

They'd talk about when they were young and what their parents used to tell them. How they hunted and where they hunted. Whatever they did. And they'd talk about much older people, before them. They used to tell where they lived and where they hunted.

Also, they would tell about people from far away who used to come down for potlatch and for good times. They would talk about those people's ways of doing things. How they did a lot of things much different from the people around here. Like they built their canoe different, and their boats, different and so on.

Far as I can remember, fellow by the name of Young Toby was one of the last old ones to pass away. He used to tell quite a bit of stories. I liked to listen to him. He especially used to tell us about one year when he went beaver hunting with his father in the spring.

They used to hike out quite a ways up on the flats. He told us about how he just had thirty-three shells. He talked about that quite a bit. Thirty-three rifle shells he took along and out of that thirty-three he got thirty-two beaver. He just missed one. Probably he was a good shot, I don't know. But in them years they just knew how to hunt them beavers.

Then this Young Toby got sick out there. That's quite a ways from where they were hunting. I'd say about twenty-five miles. His old man, they called him Old Toby, had to pack him that far back home. That's one of the stories he used to tell.

Real Trapping With My Old Man

First I start trapping small game like weasels, squirrels and snare rabbits. Sometimes I'd go out little ways with my mother looking at her traps, then I'd walk back to camp. She'd tell me to go on home and she'd keep going to her traps.

When I was about fourteen, that's the first time I start to go out trapping. Real trapping with my old man. There was quite a few marten in that year. He used to go out with me just a little ways to show me how it was done. Later on we'd move to the next camp about six miles up further. Then we started another line. This time I do it alone myself. I never used to go very far. That was my start of trapping.

So as I grew older, everytime my old man and I go out trapping together when it snows heavy he used to walk ahead and I would handle sleigh. I was about sixteen or seventeen years old at that time. In some instances he used to go packing out. No dogs, just packing three or four days. I used to be along with him and he'd show me how things were done. How to make camp and which direction to go for certain type of game. Like in them years he show me where to set the traps for marten. In a creek or in a bunch of timber. He taught me that.

Later on he told me that I just had to make a go at it myself. Camping out. I was about eighteen when I first camped out all alone. It felt lonely at first but then he told me, "You just have to take it. It's part of life you get used to."

It was an outdoor life like everybody else. We used to do as we pleased out there. That's what we liked about it. It was lot of fun moving along with dogs. That was part of life. That was about the time I got my own team. And we just keep moving, going out. We couldn't lay around waiting for it to warm up. We'd travel in any weather except when it's too warm and soft. Dogs can't travel then.

Sometimes if it's too cold, like say fifty or sixty below, and we're at

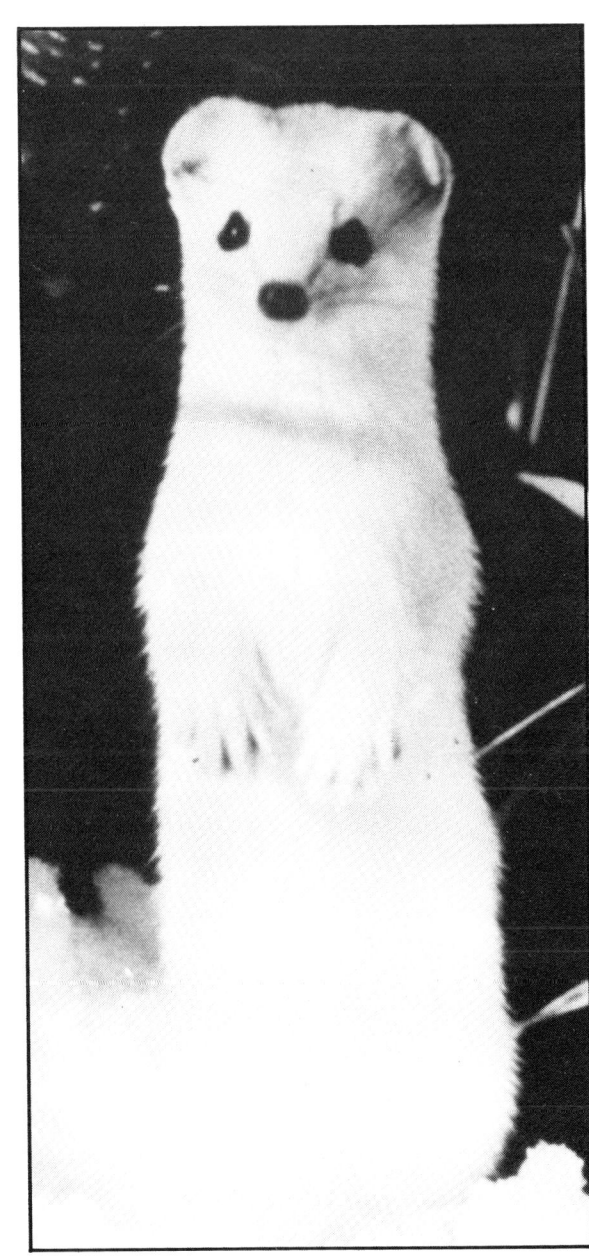

our main camp, we stay home. But if we're out with our tents where we're trapping we have to keep moving.

Lots of times I would be trapping for marten. For bait mostly we used rabbit's foot and dried fish. We used to tie it together. My old man showed me that when I start trapping with him. Then as the years came along we'd mostly use dry fish.

Other people used decayed meat. They'd use whatever's got a strong smell to it. For the last four or five years I been trapping I use this fish roe. I put it in a can in the summer and let it rot to make a strong smell. I put it in a baking powder can and broke it into little pieces. I just pour a little of that for bait. Marten could smell it from a long ways.

Some men would keep some meat in the house where it's warm. Let it spoil and get quite a strong smell. They'd cut it up and use that for marten bait too. And moose lungs, they're colored red. They'd use that. Oh anything for bait, even red paper. Marten thinks it meat or something. Even red ribbon they use.

Springtime

In the springtime, like I said, people used to come down to sell what fur they catch. We'd come down about March 15th and go back around April 5th or later we'd come to our main cabin there, April 20th or 25th we'd move out to spring camp about three miles further out. Then we'd settle there at the camp waiting for the rats to come out. After so long it turns warm and they come out to feed.

After we're through rat hunting we'd move out to the river by little poling boat. We'd make couple trips out to the river by the slough and then over portage. Then we'd hitch up our dogs and drag that boat over portage which is about 300 yards wide at this particular place. Right over.

Of course we would make loads of our stuff on the sleigh and have the dogs pull that over the portage to where they brought the boat. Relay trip. Then we're out on the river and would move out to the mouth of Kateel.

We'd stay at the mouth of Kateel just hunting around. Hunting more rats. And we used to watch people come down. They all come down the Koyukuk in the spring in their boats. They'd come to camp with us, tell us all the news, how they been doing. We knew all the people since they were from the next village. It used to be pretty good up there from what I heard. Around Huslia game was plentiful, especially muskrat.

Flood

Between 1925 and 1937 there was little flood in the spring, just now and then. It was just over the bank and then the water would drop right down. But the big flood everybody remembers was in 1937. It snowed quite a bit that winter, from around Christmas. In the spring the country was flooded for quite awhile, maybe three weeks.

There was no land when we come out of the Koyukuk River. We were at our main camp, spring camp, when the water started coming into the flats there. We'd put everything on the high cache and move to the high ground one mile away. We'd take enough grub for three or

four days. I remember we did that two or three times with this flood. Move to high ground. Sort of an island out in the middle of the lake. I was about sixteen at the time. All of us would move to that high ground with the boat. We'd take all the dogs.

Like I say, it snowed pretty heavy that winter. An average depth after it was packed down was about four feet. Regular depth in other years is about two and a half feet of snow. So everybody knew a flood was coming. They were all ready for it. The other way it floods is if ice jams down river. But snow makes the biggest floods.

"Of course you'd tell your kids to learn as much at they can in school. Then when you take them out you just teach them what you father taught you when you were kid. Show them the same things. There's not much difference between going to school and learning this outdoor life. It's pret much the same. They learn to ma a living."

Caching Ducks and Geese

The other thing in spring, we'd hunt these geese. I remember the years when there used to be a lot of white geese up here in Alaska. I'd say around 1929. There was lots on this Koyukuk River. Even my old grandfather used to like to hunt them. He'd get many. In them years they used to hunt mostly in canoes.

Their canoes couldn't hold so much so they cached them. Dug a hole on the bar, throw the geese all in there and then cover it over with brush. That would protect it for little while from other animals. Of course they'd have to come right back to get them. A bear would get to it.

In the fall they used to hunt mostly ducks. When the ducks are real fat and could hardly fly. They'd carry canoes into lakes and hunt the time of day when it's getting dark. Then the ducks could hardly see. At that time they don't pay attention. They just like to mill around along the shore feeding. The hunters could get quite a few of them like that, cache them like with the geese. Later they'd bring them home plucked and then salt them in a barrel, so they'd keep. Just like salting fish.

Fishing

After we're through rat hunting we'd come down and stay in town for about three weeks. While we're in town we'd go out and gather up logs and poles to make a fishwheel. Sometimes we'd build it here. Sometimes we'd build it when we go down to fish camp. My old man and my uncle Albert would do the building and I'd help or they'd hire help.

Roger and Hughie Jr. tying up the boat at fish camp.

Our fish camp was halfway between Koyukuk and Nulato. There was fish camps all the way along to Nulato. One or three miles apart. The fish used to be plentiful in them years. We'd catch the same amount of fish every year seems like. I remember only one year there was no fish. That was in 1939. Everybody had hard time with dog feed that winter. That's the only year I remember like that.

There was plenty of fish around Kaltag that time. But from there up this way there was hardly anything. That winter we'd have to buy corn meal or oats to mix with a little feed for dogs. Sometimes feed them rabbits. That was kind of hard without fish.

We used to bale dried salmon in a bunch. Maybe fifty, sixty in each bundle. You can just imagine how many fish it takes to feed one dog. I'd say about 250 to 300 fish a dog. That's a rough guess. An average number of dogs would be about nine a family. Forty even fifty bales would last the whole winter for about nine or ten dogs. My uncle, he wasn't married at the time, so he only had about five of his own. That's all he needed with just a small sleigh.

Just about everyone had fishwheels. Sometimes they'd go partnership on one wheel and then whatever they catch they split in half. Mostly salmon. As the summer wore on we start catching mixed fish like whitefish, and sheefish.

When the heavy run was on we'd catch lots. The most we'd cut was around 1800 fish in one day. Some camp would even catch 2000 but they couldn't handle it. But that was with a lot of different people in our camp, I'm talking about the whole camp cutting that many. The fish ran heavy for about a week. By that time we'd cut enough fish for two or three families.

Roger's sister, Jennie Pelkola, cutting king salmon. Backbones are hanging on the pole behind her.

Franklin Dayton Sr., Franklin Dayton Jr., and Elaine Solomon pulling in another king salmon across the river from fish camp.

CHAPTER FOUR   I Was Young

Airplanes

I'll tell you about my first airplane ride. It was 1939. The flier was a fellow by the name of John Cross. He was going to make a trip up to Cutoff with some freight for Dominic Vernetti. Dominic knew that I had never flown in a plane before so he asked him for me. John Cross agreed to take me along and he just charged me fifteen dollars for the round trip. Pretty cheap. Usually they charge twenty-five or thirty dollars for one way.

It was all right high in the air. Something different than traveling in a boat. I could see everything from the air. Late March. The river is way over on the left side so he didn't follow the river. I didn't get to see our winter camp. But in them years I was just young and didn't pay any attention to landmarks or anything like that.

The plane was a Stinson. Monoplane they called it. Bigger than this present day Cessna 180. There was nothing to be afraid of since a lot of people flew before me and they mentioned that they enjoyed it.

The village of Cutoff wasn't a straight stretch. We had to land way below there where the river wasn't so crooked. We made our landing and taxied about two miles to the village. Taking off was the same way, taxi about two miles to the long straight stretch. This was sort of a heavy plane this Stinson. We needed a long runway.

People don't live in Cutoff anymore. They all moved about four miles down river to what they call Huslia in about 1949. The old village site was too low, and then maybe wood was getting scarce. The

present site is much higher ground.

We didn't stay too long. Just long enough to unload. This old trader by the name of Jack Sackett invited us for a cup of tea. Then we taxied out and came back home.

Since flying was available it changed things quite a bit. Like in the years way back if you're pretty sick and have to go up to Tanana to the hospital, you have to go by boat or by dogteam. Sometimes it was too late. Whereas when planes started to become available you'd see a lot of difference there.

Also about trapping, if it snow real heavy and you had to haul quite a bit of stuff back, you'd charter an airplane to haul your stuff back. That way you'd travel with dogteam much lighter. There's a lot of changes with airplanes. Of course, you do things faster.

About 1936 - 37 was the first years that people started flying as passengers in the airplane. A regular mail flight was doing most of the freighting. From there on as planes became more available, people did more flying. At first the plane didn't land in Koyukuk. They'd fly

Hughie Kriska's cache.

Yvonne Yarber reading the manuscript for this book to Roger and Annie Dayton in their cabin at Bishop Mountain.

"I made this stove out of a barrel."

from Fairbanks down and land at Tanana and Ruby then Nulato. If you really wanted to travel someplace you'd have to be at these places. We got our mail by dogteam from Nulato up to Galena.

In 1938 a fellow by the name of Hans Miro started landing here. He was good friends with Vernettis and stayed there over night. He had a route from Fairbanks to Nome and back. Sometimes he'd do relay work. Carry so many passengers here, leave them, and go get another load. That's when flights started becoming available to us in Koyukuk.

He had his airline in operation for about three years. Then between Unalakleet and Kaltag he ran into some bad weather and crashed killing himself.

Sally Pilot's house, Joe Nelson's cache, and Ray Nelson's house.

In 1938 there was big stickdance down at Kaltag. This Wien had a route from Fairbanks to Nulato and the pilot just happened to stop here before that stickdance. A bunch of people wanted to go down there so they all asked him. He brought them down and a couple of days later he brought them back up. Whenever there's action they used to like to go by plane.

1949 I made a trip up to Fairbanks and it was $45.25, but it went much higher as the years came along.

Service

I got in the service in 1942 and out in 1946. It was like any other service, nobody liked it. I never got out of Alaska. Stayed mostly in Anchorage. Of course, some of the boys went out to the States and some went overseas, but not too many of them. Mostly I didn't like getting up at reveille, but I was young and didn't mind much.

Hughie Kriska's place, Koyukuk.

I had a couple furloughs and came back here. There weren't many changes those years. Everybody went out to camps then. Not like now when people mostly stay in town. Galena was a small village, too, just like here until they started building the air base there in 1941. At first there was a prospector who hauled galena ore out to the river with a horse right there. He'd cache it on the bank and boats would come and pick it up. They'd ply the Yukon and hauled quite a bit of this galena ore. That's how the place got its name. Of course, Koyukuk was here long before Galena ever started.

March of '43 while I was gone in the service my dad got killed. He was out on the gee pole going down a hill. The sleigh was pretty well loaded with all the winter stuff. Dogs were working hard. He ran into a tree and just happened to be in front of the sled. Of course, I never ask my mother just how it happened. What she mentioned was that his chest was all smashed in and he died instantly. It was pretty hard for my mother and pretty hard for me too because I was away from home. I thought of my mother how she was doing work all alone, taking care of the kids. But then there's always a way of doing things.

I got the army to send her some money every month, what they called allotment. I put in so much and the government would put in so much. They sent it to her and that made it easier for her.

It took me three or four days to come back here after I got out of the service. And I had to pay my own way. If the army was going to pay I'd have to wait more than a week for transportation. A bunch of us didn't want to wait, we just wanted out. So I came by flight from Anchorage to Fairbanks and by flight from Fairbanks to Galena. There was no flight down here that day so I came the rest of the way by dogteam.

It was still March and I wanted to go out beaver trapping with my uncle. He had a load going up so I had to walk all the way to our main cabin. After I spent a few days up at the main camp, I tried going one way but didn't do any good. Then I went up to where my younger brother John Jr. was trapping on the Huslia River. I tried every kind of beaver trapping and I still didn't do any good. I didn't catch not one beaver that year. There was beavers, but then I just didn't seem to catch on again. That's the difference it made being gone over three years. I forgot a few things. Like if I'd want to shoot a rabbit I'd miss it. It'd be too far. Or if I wanted to shoot a rat, spring hunting, I'd miss it. Too far away.

Gambling

After beaver season I came back in for April. Then springtime hunting rats I went up with a fellow they call Joe Nelson. Way up the Koyukuk River, he wanted me to stay with him so I spent the spring with him. The rats were pretty good price that time, anywhere from two and a half to three dollars, compared to usual seventy-five cents.

But then, since I was young, I lost it all in gambling. Whatever I caught. I suppose I didn't care. Poker. I lost it in poker right here in Koyukuk. Of course, I didn't know much about poker playing either. Just went in for the fun of it I suppose. I didn't know when to stop. I just kept right on going. But since I was single, it didn't bother me at all.

In early years there used to be big games. They'd never use chips then, they'd use straight cash, mostly coins. Right after rat hunting, piles of rats, they'd use that. Spring we'd move out to the Koyukuk River and people coming down used to stop at our camp and they'd get in a game of poker. They bet with whatever they had.

They say up in Huslia there used to be big games. People were pretty much hustlers up there. Game was abundant and people even used to bet with their furs like mink. Whenever they'd come down here they just get into big games. Or make a big game out of whatever they had.

John Nelson was a pretty lucky card player and I suppose there were two or three others but long ago I was too young to know. I remember people out close to the bank with a big canvas stretched out, mostly coins and bills and a big pile of rats in the middle.

They used to have dances for entertainment with violin or

Joe Nelson's house in Koyukuk during a snow storm.

guitar. Whoever plays violin would play night after night. Same way with the guitar player and now and then accordian. Now lot of kids play guitar. Just grab any guitar and learn pretty fast. Mostly now they have this twisting. Hardly have fox trots or waltz any more. Fox trot, one step, square dance, Virginia reel and schottische. Old people used to really enjoy that, and baseball, besides this gambling.

Dog Race

In the winter when everybody comes down together they put up a dog race. Invite other villages to come in and challenge them. A fellow from Galena named George Jimmy used to do a lot of the winning. And Joe Stickman from Nulato had a pretty good team.

Even Joe Stickman was partially disabled in one leg and he won. While these other men help their dogs along by running he just would ride on the back. And still he won. In 1928 I remember he won the Fairbanks race. The sixty mile one. He beat his younger brother who was able to run. Other racers could run up the hill but he had to ride. I guess he just trained his dogs so well they gave all they could.

They had snowshoe races and ski races too. That ski race was rough. If you ever fall down it was hard to get up again. Coming down the bank across there near everyone took a spill. I've seen them use as much as five dogs but that's hard to handle. Mostly you had to know how to handle your rope. They'd have a long rope about twenty feet long and just before going down the bank you have to play it out to slow you down. And especially around quick curves you have to gather up your rope and let it out. The towline slows down but not the

Joe Stickman, well known dog racer, coming out of church in Nulato. Photo by Father Jette.

dogs. That's the trick in that ski race. Some men start playing out their rope too late and they tumble over.

Bear

The only time I caught a bear out by myself was in 1947. I wasn't hunting bear then, I just came up to it. I was looking for a trail to trap up the Kateel River about eleven miles. We had a cabin there and I was going northeast looking for a trail around the hills where my parents used to trap. It was before freeze up. I packed ax and gun and figured to be out two or three nights camping. I was following the ridge and I came to a lump.

I see a pile of mud in front and I knew right away it was bear. I got out my pack right away and I had this 30-30 rifle with me. I went over right away, looked in there, and I see big bear head. He was looking at me. He was awake. Right away I just took a shot at it. Hit him in the eye and killed him instantly. And well, my first thought, the first thing to do is kill him right away, if you can. That's what I did.

But I couldn't get him out. It was sort of flat there. They usually have their bear hole entrance down the side of a creek and you get them out easy that way. All you got to do is pull them. But pulling upwards is pretty hard. So what I did is cut a hole out on top. Opened it up all the way to the entrance. But I couldn't roll it. It was so big of a bear I could hardly move it. I could move it side to side and try to push, get behind and try to shove. I couldn't get it. I couldn't move it. I even used my belt. Put it around his neck. I got a long pole and try to pry him out but all I did was break up my belt. Then I thought of a trick that might work.

I thought to myself suppose I lay two long poles right across the entrance where it was a little bit lower. It was narrow and the bear couldn't fall either way. I kind of stood him up and rolled him over. Head over heels. That's the only way I got him out.

I could have cached him there, but instead I packed it all in. I made four or five trips those couple miles back to my cabin. I had a regular pack sack and I filled it up with the fat first. That fat alone must have weighed eighty pounds. Lots of times we used to handle fifty pounds and the fat weighed more than that. I remember my pack straps just cutting into my shoulders. That's the heaviest part of the bear I packed in.

I told my mother about it and she told me "Why didn't you do it the easy way. Why didn't you cache it there and then haul it with dogs?" That would have been easier but I never thought of that. I didn't have dogs with me at that time. I left them with my folks at our main cabin back on the Koyukuk River. After the lakes froze good I walked back down and got my dogs. 1947, I was twenty-six then.

Roger with moose forelegs hanging outside his house in Koyukuk.

Loose Dogs

One spring I was hunting moose across from the village on the island. There was a bunch of dogs loose over there and it was a good thing. If it weren't for them I would never had got this moose. Moose will never run if a dog is chasing him. It'll just stand in one place. I've caught three moose like that.

It so happened I was going around the bank on the other side of the island here when I heard four dogs howling. Right away I know what it was so I tied my dogs right there and got my snowshoes on. Those four or five dogs had the moose stopped. First I chased the dogs away with a big stick. Pretend like I was going to hit them. They all took off. Then when the dogs left, this moose started going. He didn't get too far. I had just one good chance at it and I shot him. As I butchered it up, I thought about those loose dogs. They'd come back and eat up the meat. So I built a quick cache to protect the meat. It's a good kind of cache for foxes and like that, but not for wolverine. Wolverine will always get to your cache. One way or another. You can't hardly protect anything from wolverines.

I was twenty-four or twenty-five when I got out of the service. Since my old man got killed out at camp, I started going out by myself. I did that four years. Of course it was pretty rough for one fellow. When it snows heavy you have to snowshoe ahead a day before you can move your stuff. After I got married we went out together and it was a lot easier.

Slush ice running in the Koyukuk River between Koyukuk village and the island.

CHAPTER FIVE — Paying Bills

The Same Life

Annie in November.

In the fall of '49 I got married. Then it was the same thing over and over again. After we'd get through fishing we'd move back here to town. Everybody had boats with inboard motors in them years and we all piled up everything in there. Our groceries. We never paid for groceries, but we'd get credit from the stores. Then all our belongings, all our dogs, we'd move that up to camp for trapping. Like everybody else.

So after I got married we just had the same life. Go out trapping. Of course I had extra passenger on the sleigh. And while I went out trapping, beaver especially, she'd stay home. We had a tent there and she would cook. Sometimes I'd come home late and everything would be ready. I didn't have to cook dog food when I came home, or food for myself. I had good help like that.

I was twenty-eight and she was pretty young. Annie, that's my wife's name. Annie Yatlin. Her parents were Quentin and Tilda. They both passed away before we ever got married. Her father met with an accident and froze. A couple years later her mother passed away.

Her father was from Nulato. After he got married he moved up here to Koyukuk. Her mother was from here, the oldest in the family. There was quite a few of them but they all passed away.

That was a big family and not one of them living now except one boy and he was adopted out. I suppose her parents had too many kids and then gave him away. He was raised by a man and wife named Bazook till they passed away. Then somebody else took him for about five years until he got married. George, he's the only one left of that family. He's up in Galena now.

So I never got to really spend any time with Annie's folks because like I said, they passed away before we ever got married. They did most of their fishing down about Four Mile on the other side of the Yukon River. In fall they moved to Nicholia Slough to trap. They spent one summer at our Nine Mile fish camp, 1935. That's the only time they were around.

Fishing

Some years Annie's folks would stay up a Bishop Rock for the fall for fishing. That was before we start to go there. Many different people fished there ahead of us. One of them was Charlie Evans from Galena. People before him, well they just came down through the years.

In the first place it used to belong to nobody. Someone would fish here and then they get tired of the place and move away. Then somebody else would come here. There used to be a regular fish camp across on the other side from where we are now. Then the people used to camp on this side and have a fishwheel around the bluff.

In the late 1890s there used to be them miners coming from Outside. The only thing they could turn to a few dollars was to cut wood for the steamers plying the Yukon up and down. During that time quite a bit of wood was cut in the area. There used to be a mail cabin there too.

A fellow by the name of Jack Mongahan built a cabin back in the

Agnes Derendoff, Mrs. Malemute-*Biyeedohudinaadaghot*, Arthur (in front), Quenten Malemute, Gregory Malemute, Alex Malemute. Photo taken in Nulato by Father Jette.

lake from Bishop Rock where people used to trap. He didn't cut wood, just stayed out. Later when he left the place other people used it as a trapping place. I myself was there one year just for a visit. Then in later years it was mostly used as a fish camp.

Around 1890 there was a bishop, Bishop Seghers, killed there. He was camping there for awhile going on down the river. His companion got out of his mind and then killed this bishop. There was nobody else there at the time. These other missionaries from Nulato shipped his body back Outside. So that was how the place Bishop Mountain got its name.

We started going to Bishop Rock to fish around '52 or '53. First we were down at Nine Mile. Used to be good fishing. For some reason it tapered off quite a bit. We'd move our fishwheels here and there but it don't seem to do any good. What I found out is the fish ran on the outside of the island and then they'd come into shore about three miles further up. So the site down there was no good anymore. From that time on we start fishing at Bishop Rock.

Mostly we'd fish for king salmon with a fishwheel. The whole family and two or three other families. We'd put up eating fish. We're so used to eating fish that we have to go out and catch as much as we can for the winter. We lived there through the summer and stayed there through the fall. We'd fish whitefish under the ice and then move back to town between the 8th and 15th of November. After that start out to trap from our main camp before Christmas.

I never did that ice fishing since I start working for the school The kids mostly go for moose meat over fish. Right now Marion Huntington is fishing for whitefish a little above the bluff. Then at Bishop Rock my brothers Franklin and John Dayton are fishing like that.

Setting the net under the ice.

Madeline Solomon looking through birchbark collected by her grandchildren. She'll make baskets out of the best pieces.

Out With Annie and The Kids

I was trapping in them years we first got married. We went out together for about four years I believe. Then Annie stayed home with our firstborn child, second and third and so on. We couldn't really go out with them. It was too cold. And after they started going to school she stayed here in town like the rest of the women. Parents that had children going to school had to go out from town trapping.

People had no choice but stay in the village on account of their kids. They went out little ways up the Koyukuk River. And they hunted, people that stayed in the village. But we never went out any more rat hunting. In the summer there was hardly anybody in the village. Everybody went out to their camps fishing. Before this school, nobody would stay in town for the trapping season.

When Annie start to stay in town with the kids I had to go out to our main camp. I had everything up there except my groceries and a little fish. In that way I didn't have much load when I started out from here. Of course I was using dogteam.

The first child was a girl, born in 1950. Rita, she's over in Anchorage now going to some kind of training. We'd take her out and bundle her up good and make sure she's warm in the sleigh. Sometimes it gets cold in the tent and we'd have to see to it that she doesn't get cold. Wrap her in these Hudson Bay wool blankets and keep the fire going. In the old days they used to use rabbitskin blankets which was much lighter and warmer. But nowadays you never see them anymore.

I remember going out with three children and then after that we

Annie cutting king salmon with a *tłabaas*.

didn't go out too much with the fourth child. But he was born out on the Kateel River that was the last time trapping out there. I had to be the midwife on that fourth child born. We could have come down here but I didn't want to lose too much time traveling. Everybody understood that. We had so much big bill to pay.

That was maybe twenty-two years since that fourth child was born. Like I say, I could have brought Annie down here but I had a lot of beaver trapping to do. That year I still couldn't pay up my bill with the store. Then a good thing, next summer I went to work at Galena for construction with Peter Kiewit. They were going to repave that whole airfield. I worked as a laborer, $3.48 an hour. That was big money to us in them years. That's the way I got out of it all, paid my bills. That fall I paid for my groceries with a little left over.

That's the first year I ever did that, a good year for me. Everybody else that was lucky enough to work did the same thing. That's when trapping sort of tapered off, since the people start working by the hour.

So I left my family in town from that time on. We had nine children all together. The last one born was in 1965. She's thirteen now. We never had any more after that. One daughter lives with her boyfriend up in Anaktuvik Pass where he's working. She had a daughter. And my son who's twenty-six has a little girl. That makes two grandchildren that I've got.

Storm on the Yukon can swamp these boats easily. Roger reties them for safety and props them away from the bank with a pole.

Big Bills

1963 was the last time I trapped out on the Kateel River. I went out alone and would start from here at Koyukuk and go all the way up to our main camp. It's fifty miles from here to our main camp. And from there up the Kateel River for another thirty-five miles trapping marten. That's the furthest I went.

Sometimes it was a tough time from here. Especially if it snowed too much. We had dogteams in those years. Yeah, '63 is the longest I ever went with dogs. I did pretty good that year but like I said, we had a lot of bills in them years. Big bills. And we had to pay that.

We got everything from here for the whole winter. It all had to go on the book. Sometimes the storekeeper here would let our credit run over $1000. It depends on who you are and where you're trapping. Maybe a few people were over $2000. But I've never heard of anybody going over $2000 from here.

When you sell your furs to the store and there's something left over after you pay the bill, they never give you cash. Hardly ever. Like this Dominic's store. He had special coins that was good only for his store. They call them bingles. They were from quarter to a dollar and then up to five dollars. This brass bingle that was the size of a quarter was worth five dollars.

The other store they used to call Johnny Evans' used to handle bingles too. And that was only good for his trade. In that way you'd do business with only one store. Finally they did away with those

Cache at Bishop Mountain.

bingles. They're antiques now.

This guy Joe Notti used to have a little store up Koyukuk River. He handled them bingles too. I heard he had a fifty cent piece. He was offered a thousand dollars for it but wouldn't sell it. So whoever got them now is worth a lot of money.

Dominic Vernetti

The last time I worked for Dominic was in 1960, cutting wood, bringing stuff from the warehouse and bringing in ice. Sometimes getting behind the counters and selling a few things. That's the only time I work for him.

In the summertime he's got lots of men to work for him when his freight comes. I worked quite a bit longshoring for him. We'd unload things right into the warehouse. Sometimes he'd hire the older people to make a little log cabin or repair his house.

Dominic's store had everything. General merchandise from little nails, washtubs, traps, shovels, inboard motors and food. Nowadays stores don't handle too much of that. Like for dogteams he used to handle webbing, ropes, snaps, rings. Tools, files, hammers, everything he used to handle.

He was quite a guy, an Italian. He used to tell about when he first came into this country. Boy he did a lot of hard work. He was in the service in Italy and deserted to come to the United States. He started out mining and sometimes sink a hole where there's nothing. His means of travel was three dogs and he'd never ride, always walk. But it didn't bother him. He was young.

He got into the store business through another storekeeper. He worked for him running a store. Then after he made so much he started his own. That's how he got the business. And you can't beat a kind-hearted man like him. If you're broke or were from someplace else and wanted to go home he'd send you home. He'd help you anytime. Of course sooner or later you'd have to pay him back. And sometimes, well you know how business people are, they like to make extra money. Oh yeah.

Like during beaver trapping you'd have to watch him measure the beaver. Sometimes he'd pull that tape a little towards him and undersize the beaver that way by one or two inches. But then some people used to get the best of him and hold the tape about two or three inches on their side.

But then he'd never let you down. He was the only man I know of that would never let you down. If he knows you're stuck or broke or just passing through he'd help you. And he'd watch you at the same time to see if you done good trapping. He'd see to it that you used your money to buy your stuff. He won't give you too much credit if you have money.

And if you did good with beavers he'd make sure you paid your store bill. Then whatever extra you would leave in the store. He'd be careful to give you just so much cash in later years when they did away with those bingles. But like I say, he would help you anytime.

Yeah, he was quite a guy. I remember in '63 we had the highest flood I can remember. There was an ice jam downriver and it forced this ice and water right over the banks. All that time Dominic stayed with his store.

All the women and children were evacuated by helicopter. Before the last load we moved on top of the church, all the men and what women they couldn't take. When the helicopter finally came for old lady Sally Pilot they lowered the basket. She was pretty scared with that basket swinging back and forth and turning around.

All the men stayed on top of the church about three nights. We played a little cards, poker and took turns cooking. The army left C-rations with us and maybe someone would take a boat and shoot a duck or two for soup. We had outboard motors and would use them to go feed our dogs which we kept on rafts.

We'd have to make our way through the ice. It was mostly small pieces that came further back over the bank. Of course it was kind of rough to start feeding the dogs. They'd get too excited. They'd jump over the side of the raft and you'd have to pull them on again. I made a tank raft for my six dogs.

During that flood Dominic stayed with his store. And when the flood went over his first floor he moved upstairs. Then that water kept coming up until it was a foot over the second floor. That's how high the water was. When the flood ended there was about a quarter inch of mud in every house that we had to clean out.

My house, well it lifted up and drifted out of place. I built that one in '57 and my boy is living in it. Even today it sits in the place where it drifted. There was about four or five houses that drifted, including the community hall.

Cannery Work

From about 1957 I started trapping from here where they call the Big Portage. After we fish a little up at Bishop Rock the family would come back to town and I'd go out from here in the fall. I did that for eight or nine years. Then after we start going down to the cannery like the other boys here I didn't have to go out too much trapping. Except for beaver. That was when trapping really tapered off.

First time I ever went to the cannery was '46. There were lot of different types of work there. You would be a head butcher, or a fish inspector to check for any bones or guts, or a slimer who cleans fish, what the machines don't clean. That's all work in the processing plant on the ground floor. You'd work all the way down the line till the fish came out in cases.

Most of the time the canning shop was up on the next floor. And there we'd be strung out all along doing different types of work. Some would be shoveling bunch of coolers with cans into the big boilers and on the other end someone would be pulling them out after they're in there for an hour and a half. Some would be driving Jitneys and hauling the cans to where they cool off. Then twenty-four hours later they'd haul them to the casing line.

After the fishing and canning was over, season closed, we'd do a lot of longshoring. We'd load these tenders as much as it could hold and these open scows would haul them out to the ship. You'd have to longshore on the docks or handle the cases on the ship.

Working on the ship was pretty rough work. Sometimes it got pretty rough and they'd have to turn the tenders loose from the ship. When the strong winds come up they wouldn't be tied alongside the ship to be unloading.

Sometimes you wouldn't sleep for days. They couldn't afford to lose any time. A ship will hold about 300,000 cases and didn't have much time to be anchored there. You'd have to load that ship no matter how tired you were. They just keep you piling cases, either from the cannery to the scow or from the scow to the ship. Longshoring. The first time I ever went out, I don't think we slept ten hours in five days. There was no replacements. That's the roughest life I ever had.

I'd say longshoring out on the ship was the hardest job. Whenever you're outside along the ship in the scow, or in the hold. Sometimes scow after scow would come to the ship for loading. Maybe you could rest a little while on the ship but there'd be no sleep.

If you were working for the ship, you'd be down in the hold. If you're working for the cannery you'd be outside on the scow. Down in the hold was better for me. I tried a few times out on the scow but, gee whiz, I couldn't stand it. I'd just get seasick. People of the Interior just couldn't stand that rough weather out there, the waves being so high and everything rocking. Sometimes fishermen get drowned in that sort of weather. But they seem to go out in any sort of weather.

Even with longshoring there'd be accidents. You have to watch out loading, with a load of cases overhead. If one happens to spill down in the hold you have to get out of the way. That's one thing they always told us. They were careful, them people on the ship. Especially the winchmen, they see that you'd be out of the way before they let the load down into the hold. I didn't see hardly any accidents.

One thing though, when you work you just keep going. The machine don't stop. Like if you're feeding lids on the cans up in the canning shop you have to keep up. Same way down below in the processing plant. You'd have to feed the fish to the head butcher. The next guy feed it to what they call the iron chink, it rips open the fish and cleans out the guts. The machine don't stop. You have to keep up with it.

They paid pretty good. They were paying cash at that time, and overtime. Then after a while they started paying us in checks. The cannery didn't trust any boys getting drunk or gambling their money away. I remember when they pay us all in cash we all got into a big game of dice. Some of the boys came home broke. That news went all over the cannery and then, like I said, they paid in checks after that.

Sometimes they never gave you checks until you came home. They'd give it all to one guy to have in his possession and then he'd pass out the checks once everybody get home. I guess lately they never did that. But people from around here quit going to the cannery after fire fighting jobs started around here. The last time we ever went to the cannery was about '69 or '70. I guess the cannery recruiter knew what was going on and quit coming around to pick up cannery boys. Then they started hiring mostly men from the States, Filipinos. I guess that's who they hire mostly nowadays. They were pretty well experienced in cannery work, them people.

1960 was our first job down in Bristol Bay. About six or seven men from here would go, whoever was able to. You weren't allowed to work until you were eighteen. We'd be gone as long as a month and a half, depending on how the fish ran, whether they were light or heavy. And in that way we would get unemployment benefits to help us along after we finished with the season. Then we didn't have to go out

Garden at fish camp.

trapping before Christmas when it's so dark.

Then after Christmas we'd go out beaver trapping like everybody did. That was from 1960 till around 1969 everybody did that. That's when this fire fighting work came up and everybody quit going to the canneries. Of course it's not every year that you go fire fighting, it's just whenever they call you.

While we're out at the cannery our wives would live in town here. Sometimes they'd be out in fish camps fishing king salmon mostly. They'd make strips or put them in a barrel or cut them as eating fish. They would be doing that while the men are in the cannery.

Of course all during that time life was changing. Trapping was tapering off and most of the time families would just stay in town. I never did take my boys out trapping yet since I start working down here in school. I start working about ten years ago and then I never did go out trapping any more. I work as a custodian here for the school. This is my tenth year. I had this surgery and had to lay off for awhile, but I'm back at it again. Working here at the school.

Annie in June repairing the net.

CHAPTER SIX   Koyukuk 1979

Teaching Kids About Outdoor Life

Gabriel is fifteen now and I'm starting to take him out to show him a few things in the woods. I never really hiked out with him too long. Just lately I started going out with him to show how things was done. Still too warm yet. This morning I told him there would be a lot of water along the river and the creek wouldn't freeze too good. That's where I went in, one side leg through the ice. We talked about that.

And I also talked about handling traps in this warm weather. Your traps will become all wet. And then walking through the woods your legs would get wet. And talking about trapping. I just showed him how to set a trap. If he was lucky enough to get anything, I'd just show him how to skin that marten and stretch it on the dryer.

We talk about things like in cold weather if you sweat you never take your clothing off. You just stayed one place until you cool off. Otherwise if you work up a sweat and take your clothes off you might catch pneumonia. In really cold weather you don't have to wait long to stop sweating anyway.

But warm weather like now I always take six or seven pairs of gloves. I used to set about seven traps with the first pair of gloves no matter how wet it was. That way I'd have enough dry gloves. What gets wet on you is your gloves because you're handling traps and then you're cutting poles and cutting toggles. Of course, your legging gets pretty wet too in soft weather. If we get too wet out there we build a fire and dry up a little bit.

So today I went through the ice, but I expected that. Maybe I just wanted to convince my boy that the creeks would thaw out in warm weather. He was just bugging me but I figured I'd better let him find out for himself.

The overflow was a little bit deep on the river and then we came up to Andrew Paul Slough. Now in warm weather that side of the slough, whatever already freeze, just all thaws out and the water starts running again. At a certain crossing, the one place where we turn around, I knew the ice wasn't very thick. So I stopped my machine there, got my ax out, and started going across the creek.

I test the ice with my ax, but just about in the middle one side of my leg went through. Couple days ago I went over the same spot but the ice was frozen enough to hold me up. Warm weather like this the ice will get thin and places will open up again. I've mentioned that to him, but then he's so young and maybe we were all the same way, just didn't believe our parents.

That's one thing I told him. When it gets too warm it's just no use to go out at all. The snow will get so soft that if you're snowshoeing lot of snow would be packed on your snowshoes and they'd become heavy. So most likely, everybody stayed home in this sort of weather. But sometimes kids won't believe anything and the best way is just to show them. Well I showed him all right when I went through the ice.

He'll probably go out weekends but if he already has his traps set out he might ask the teacher for an afternoon off to go around the line. Most of the time the teacher will let him go because it's part of his learning, too. Sometimes he might make a quick run around a short

"These are my son Dugal's dogs. The doghouse is just like what I used to have." 1978.

line back here two or three miles because he has a snow machine and can make the trip in just a short while.

We gave up having dogs before Gabriel start remembering so he's not much interested. He drove one or two before but like everybody else he's just interested in snow machines. You hardly ever see anybody go out with dogteam anymore. Just maybe two or three guys and the rest use the snow machine.

In the fall of '69 I bought my first snow machine. Other people got one earlier say around '62. A fellow bought that first one in Fairbanks and shipped it over but it was a different type. It was called a "Snowtraveler" with little tracks right in the middle and runners ran all the way back on both sides. Now you see both skis right in front and the track behind.

You cover more country with a snow machine than with a dog team. You can do in one day what a team might do in two or three days. But if we had snow machines forty years ago there might not be any fur around now. You could cover your area in less time, but then you'd make a longer run and if you break down you have to walk. Way out there's no parts, no gas. I'd say with a dogteam it was much better way out in the bush. All you need is your dog feed then no matter how cold it is you could travel with the dogteam.

Sometimes it's hard to warm up a snow machine to get it started. I use a little gas stove and a stove pipe to throw some heat up the carburetor. And you just can't get into overflow with a snow machine. Snow gets packed up between the track. If it's real cold you have to make a fire and thaw it out. A dogteam could just go right through overflow and it wouldn't bother them at all.

Snowmachine on the backstreet of Koyukuk.

The school wants kids to learn about outdoor life, too. A couple years ago they took all the boys out for the night just about this time in the fall. The kids seem to enjoy it. Nothing is too hard. The person who is in charge will see to it that they didn't work hard, or lift too heavy or go too far. And they see to it that they stayed off where they think the ice was thin. They showed them just how to make camp and the kids seem to enjoy it. I suppose they like to be away from school now and then.

Teaching kids about the outdoor life you have to teach each one. You expect the first one to know what you taught him but of course he will make a mistake now and then like we all were. One of the hardest things is how to make a sled. You have to go hunting for good straight grain birch. Then hew it and plane it and let it dry for a couple weeks. Since my family start staying in town going to school I've never built too many sleds, never taught them anything about that. The most important things I can teach them about outdoor life is hunting and trapping.

Whatever they have to learn in school you just let them go the way they're learning. Of course you'd tell your kids to learn as much as they can in school. Then when you take them out you just teach them what your father taught you when you were a kid. Show them the same thing. There's not much difference between going to school and learning this outdoor life. It's pretty much the same. They learn to make a living.

Kids that go to college and have success in learning, I suppose they can get a good job. But if they drop out and come home to live the way we live they wouldn't accomplish much with just school learning. If they took up some course and got a job in that and was successful, then I'd advise him to stay with it as long as he can. The same with trapping. If he can be successful with it, he should stay with it. Can you find much difference between the two?

To be a successful trapper the main thing is the country has got to be abundant. If there's no fur to trap, no matter how good a trapper you are, you won't have anything to catch. Being successful for anybody is to be out as long as you can away from town and tend to your trapping. Like say you go out and set a bunch of traps and it snows heavy about two or three days later. You'd have to go over your line and uncover the traps.

And being successful in trapping or hunting you have to listen quite a bit. Pay attention to what your teacher tells you. Whether it's your uncle or your father. If you learn all that he taught you then I'd call that being successful. He'd teach you just where to go if you're hunting bear. If you're lucky enough to find a bear or two then he'd consider you succcessful.

The same way with other game. If you go trapping and fur is abundant, and you do good, you've got all your furs dried and and you come in with a big bunch of fur then maybe they would consider you a success. Whereas on the other hand if game is pretty scarce, nothing to trap, that just can't be helped no matter how good of a hunter or trapper you are because it simply isn't there. The game just isn't there to harvest.

An average Native like me wouldn't care for city life. The time I was in the service I spent almost three years in Anchorage. It would be different if I was born and raised in a city. Maybe I'd like that. And if

Annie cutting moose meat

I had a job. Nowadays if you get a good job and stay with it, live in the city, maybe it wouldn't bother this younger generation. But as I grow older, I like to stay home.

Dewaine Dayton, Raymond Dayton, and Glen Kriska playing during recess in front of the school, 1978.

Bringing moose meat down from the cache.

Water in Koyukuk

I was a member of the council in '64 and '65. But I was just acting as first councilman because the main councilman was up Galena working. He put me in his place and that's the only time I was on the town council. That time we had a meeting about building a community center. We agreed that all the men would go out and cut so many logs and whenever they bring them in we all help pull them up the bank. We all agreed that we'd start building right away not even let the logs dry just start building. That's what a councilman does. He gets all the people together especially for certain events like dog races, snowshoe races, dinner for a potlatch, and getting wood for the community hall.

They have a meeting and talk about what events to have and who will be timekeeper and sargent-at-arms and what order to have events. But the council didn't have anything to do with the new laundry and water plant.

Two or three people came to discuss the new laundry from the government and a lot of us were against it. I spoke against it. We did our own washing up in our own washtubs. After that laundry got built and after so long it would be turned over to us and we'd have to stand the cost of the operation. And we couldn't afford all the fuel for the generators and all that. That's what we thought and that's why we were against it.

When we have a meeting they talk about putting electricity around the village but from what I understand it will cost us about $30-35,000.

We'd have to stand that cost. We'd have to buy the wire and hire an electrician to install the panel in the powerhouse. We'd have to buy these transformers and that would come to about $30-35,000. That's a lot for this village.

Water from the water plant seems a little too hard. Some people drink it, but I myself couldn't stand it for very long because it sort of dries up my mouth. And then it gets the pots pretty black. But it's good for washing and I haul it by the barrel after we run low.

Summer we get our water from the river and in the fall we cut blocks of ice out from a lake back behind the village. Last fall I went out with Gary the school teacher to cut ice because he wanted to learn how to do it. We worked for a couple hours and cut about fifty blocks. Each one was about two hundred pounds but they're easy to handle when you use ice tongs to pull it out.

The way my father taught me to do it you cut with an ax first about three inches deep. Then you cut one end and put the saw in. Big flat saw. The thinner the ice the faster you can cut. You don't saw for the cross cuts because that's just a waste of time. You just mark it with the ax then break it off. We drag it out of the hole and stand it up back by the edge of the lake so overflow wouldn't come and freeze it down again.

Signs of Luck

About three years ago my wife and I were going down to play cards. Just out where the road turns in the direction towards the village we saw a bright light. It was all colors. It was green, yellow and sort of blue like a rainbow. Just coming in this direction not really going by, just floating. Then when it was over the river it just went out. We really saw it and some kids saw it, too. It wasn't flying just sort of drifting. I don't know what it was. Then it went out just like a light going out.

Something like that happened to me out on the trapline one winter. I started out early about six o'clock with a candle light. I wanted to come home early and move down to the next camp. About a mile from the camp there was something bright just came behind me. So bright I could just see my shadow. I thought the moon came up. But when I looked back I didn't see anything at all. I didn't think nothing of it. I was just young. I just kept going on the line there. I didn't really see the light so it must have gone out before I turned around. Some people think that's a sign of bad news.

They include that with a lot of other things, signs. Like if you go out hunting and you don't get anything that's a sign of bad luck. That happened to my grandfather one fall. My uncle and my old man and somebody else went out hunting. They saw nine bears throughout the fall and didn't get one of them. Then that winter my grandfather passed away. My grandfather said himself that's not too good. Sort of bad luck, a sign like something will happen. Of course, there's other signs but I wouldn't really know.

For good luck mostly you have to dream about it. Like if you see someone in your dream when you're all alone sure enough they come visit you from another camp.

My grandfather was lucky all his life with trapping and there was one sign in particular. He was out hunting with his father, my great-grandfather, and during the day when he left camp a weasel got in his

bedding and had young ones in there. When he found them he was going to throw them all away but my great-grandfather told him no. It's not right. If you skin all of them you'll be lucky all of your life. Well I guess the best he could do was skin most of it, maybe about four. Then he couldn't skin the rest. My old man used to tell me that was an indication of good luck and grandfather was sort of lucky all his life. Of course there are other indications, but it happens so many ways.

For the past ten years I haven't heard things that indicate good luck coming. Naturally you have to be older to talk about that. All I could say to young people who don't know about this luck is, think things over. If you happen to be out alone and come to something that's pretty hard, don't rush. Like if you come to a stream with snow machine and want to cross, check the ice first. Don't try to do everything in one day. I used to do that a lot and just tire myself out for nothing.

One old timer came up to me when I was young and building a cache in Koyukuk. He asked how I was doing. I told him it was taking so long it was just disgusting. He was right when he told me, "If you do it too fast you might have to do it over." It's the same way for everybody. Take your time and do it right.

Index

airplanes 50-53
Anchorage 78, 79
Andrews 33
Apostolik, Charlie 35, 36
Basel 15
bear 39-41, 57, 58
Bear Creek 23
bingles 66, 67
birch 39
birth 14, 65
Bishop Mountain (Bishop Rock) 13, 49, 61-63, 70
Bishop Segers 62
cannery work 70-73
Captain Adams 36
conflicts 15-18
Cross, John 50
Cutoff 50, 51
dancing 55, 56
Dayton, Annie (Yatlin) 60, 61, 64
Dayton, Gabriel (Gabe) 40, 74, 75
Dayton, John, Jr. 21
Dayton, John, Sr. (father) 39-41, 43
Dayton, Oscar 26
Dayton, Rita 64
Dayton, Tom (grandfather) 18-20, 47
Dayton, Uncle Albert 18-21, 47, 48
Demientieffs 33
dogs 43, 44, 54, 56, 58-60
Edwards 33
Eskimo 14-19, 28
Evans, Johnny 66, 67
Evans, Wilfred 16
Fairbanks 53, 54
fishing 47-49, 61-63, 70, 73
floods 45, 46, 68, 69

Fourth of July 31, 32
Galena 23, 53, 54, 65
gambling 55
games 31-33
gee-pole 15
Hardnuts, Billy 36
Holy Cross Mission 26-37
hunting 35, 39-45, 47, 57-59
Huntington, Marion 62
Huslia 45, 55
Huslia River 14, 17, 18
Kaltag 48, 52, 53
Kateel River 16, 44, 45, 65
Kewitt, Peter 65
Koyukon (language) 26-28
Koyukuk 12, 14, 31, 32, 47, 48, 66, 80, 81
Koyukuk River 16, 41, 47, 64, 67
Koyukuk Station 23-25
Kuskokwim River 36
language 26-28
luck 81-84
Malemute, Quentin 60
McGrath 36
medicine man 20-21
military service 53-54
miners 61
Miro, Hans 52
missionaries 26-28
Miss Old Toby 21
muskrat (ratting) 22, 44, 45
Mongahan, Jack 61
Nelson, Joe 55
Nelson, John 55
Nenana (steamer) 36-37
Nicholia Slough 23
Notti, Joe 67

Noorvik 15, 18
Nulato 14, 20, 48, 52, 53, 60
old stories 15, 41, 42
Old Toby 42
Ott, Martin 30
Pilot, Andrew 20, 21
Pilot, Sally 20
potlatch 20
Rampart 24
Ruby 20, 24, 52
Sackett, Jack 51
school 26-29, 33-36, 75, 77
sled building 39, 77
snowmachine (sno-go) 76
Solomon, Madeline (mother) 14, 22, 25, 38, 42, 54, 58, 63
spring camp 45
Stickman, Joe 56
Stickman, Old Joseph 19-21
stores 22, 60, 65-69
Tanana 52
teaching kids 74-78
telephone 23-25
tobacco 15, 16
trading 19
trapping 15, 21, 22, 26, 42-44, 60, 64-66, 73-78
Vernetti, Dominic 25, 50, 67-69
village council 80
Walkers 33, 34
Walker, James 34
Walters, Dave 21
Williams, Cecelia 14
working for wages 64-66, 70-73
Yatlin, Tilda (Malemute) 60
Young Toby 42
Yukon River 20, 48

the Alaska biography series

Alaska Series

These books are designed for upper level elementary students living in rural Alaska, but they are sure to captivate readers of any age. They describe a rich and varied -though neglected - culture, and mirror the changes that have taken place in this area in an historically short period of time.

NOW AVAILABLE

Moses Henzie - Allakaket	ISBN 0-88839-061-0
Oscar Nictune - Alatna	ISBN 0-88839-062-9
Joe Beetus - Hughes	ISBN 0-88839-065-3
Henry Beatus, Sr. - Hughes	ISBN 0-88839-063-7
Frank Tobuk - Bettles	ISBN 0-88839-064-5
Madeline Solomon - Koyukuk	ISBN 0-88839-066-1
Roger Dayton - Koyukuk	ISBN 0-88839-067-X
Edwin Simon - Huslia	ISBN 0-88839-068-8
John Honea - Ruby	ISBN 0-88839-073-4